D0776770

KITCHEN CONFIDANT

kitch
confi

en
dant

**AN
INDISPENSABLE
GUIDE
FOR THE
BAKER,
DRINKER,
AND COOK**

CHRONICLE BOOKS
SAN FRANCISCO

Library of Congress Cataloging-in-Publication Data.
Title: Kitchen confidant.
Description: San Francisco : Chronicle Books, [2018] |
  Includes index.
Identifiers: LCCN 2017025015 | ISBN 9781452165189 (hc : alk.
  paper)
Subjects: LCSH: Cooking—Handbooks, manuals, etc. |
  Baking—Handbooks, manuals, etc. | Alcoholic beverages—
  Handbooks, manuals, etc.
Classification: LCC TX651 .K578 2018 | DDC 641.5—dc23 LC
  record available at https://lccn.loc.gov/2017025015

Manufactured in China

Design by **Vanessa Dina**
Illustrations by **Arthur Mount**
Typeset by **Frank Brayton**

10 9 8 7 6 5 4 3 2 1

Chronicle Books LLC
680 Second Street
San Francisco, California 94107
www.chroniclebooks.com

CONTENTS

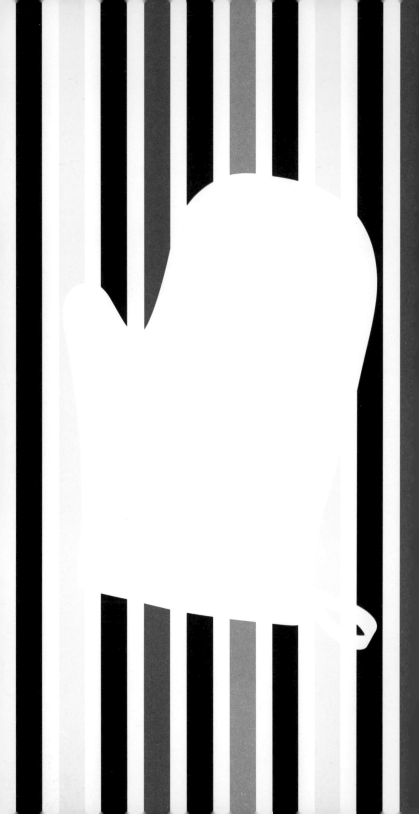

PART I

Baker's Handbook

Basic Baking Equipment

The must-haves

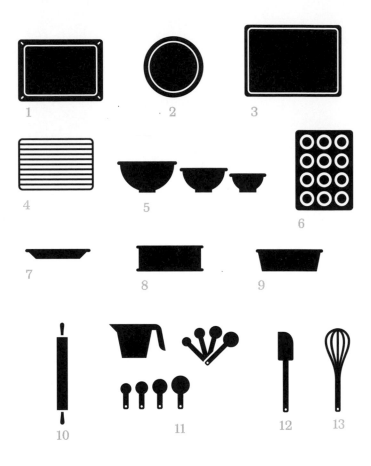

9-x-13-in [23-x-33-cm] baking dish (glass or aluminum) (1), 8- or 9-in [20- or 23-cm] round cake pan (2), cookie sheet (3), cooling rack (4), mixing bowls (at least three different sizes) (5), 12-well muffin tin (6), 9-in [23-cm] pie pan (7), 9- or 10-in [23- or 25-cm] springform pan (8), 1-lb [455-g] loaf pan (9), rolling pin (10), liquid and dry measuring cups and measuring spoons (11), spatula (12), whisk (13)

The nice-to-haves

candy thermometer (14), cookie cutters (15), food processor (16), mixer (stand or handheld) (17), oven thermometer (18), pastry brush (19), pie weights (20), ramekins (21), sifter (22), silicone baking mats (23)

Oven Temperature Conversions

Degrees Fahrenheit	Degrees Celsius
175	80
200	95
225	110
250	120
275	135
300	150
325	165
350	180
375	190
400	200
425	220
450	230
475	240
500	260
550	290

Volume Conversions

Cups and Tablespoons	Milliliters/ Liters	Fluid Ounces
¼ cup (4 Tbsp)	60 ml	2 fl oz
⅓ cup (5 Tbsp)	75 ml	2½ fl oz
½ cup (8 Tbsp)	120 ml	4 fl oz
⅔ cup (11 Tbsp)	165 ml	5½ fl oz
¾ cup (12 Tbsp)	180 ml	6 fl oz
1 cup (16 Tbsp)	240 ml	8 fl oz
2 cups (1 pt)	480 ml	16 fl oz
3 cups	720 ml	24 fl oz
4 cups (1 qt)	960 ml	32 fl oz
4½ cups	1 L	34 fl oz

Baking Pan Dimensions and Volume

When swapping from one pan to another, don't forget to adjust baking time too. Switching from one pan to multiple smaller pans or a cupcake pan will mean you will need a shorter time until the recipe is done.

Baking Pan Dimensions	Volume
8-x-1½-in [20-x-4-cm] round cake pan	5 cups [1.2 L]
8-x-2-in [20-x-5-cm] round cake pan	7 cups [1.7 L]
9-x-2-in [23-x-5-cm] round cake pan	9½ cups [2.3 L]
9-x-2½-in [23 x 6 cm] springform	10 cups [2.4 L]
12-well standard muffin pan (2¾-x-1½-in [7-x-4-cm] wells)	6 cups (½ cup per well) [1.4 L (120 ml per well)]
24-well mini muffin pan (2-x-1⅛-in [5-x-3-cm] wells)	6 cups (¼ cup per well) [1.4 L (60 ml per well)]
9-x-13-x-2½-in [23-x-33-x-6-cm] baking pan	17¾ cups [4.2 L]
8-x-8-x-2¼-in [20-x-20-x-5.5-cm] baking pan	9¼ cups [2.2 L]
9-x-9-x-2¼-in [23-x-23 x 5.5-cm] baking pan	11¾ cups [2.8 L]
8½-x-3¾-in [21.5-x-9.5-cm] Bundt pan	9¾ cups [2.3 L]
10-x-3½-in [25-x-9-cm] Bundt pan	12 cups [2.8 L]
1-lb [455-g] (8½-x-4½-x-2¾-in [21.5-x-11-x-7-cm]) loaf pan	6½ cups [1.5 L]
1½-lb [680-g] (10-x-5-x-3-in [25-x-12-x-7.5-cm]) loaf pan	9¼ cups [2.2 L]
Standard (9-x-1¼-in [23-x-3.5-cm]) pie pan	4½ cups [1 L]
Deep-dish (9½-x-1⅝-in [24-x-4.5-cm]) pie pan	6¾ cups [1.6 L]

Metric Conversions for Common Ingredients

If you prefer to weigh your ingredients in grams, but your recipes are based on volume (cups), or vice versa, this handy chart will help you figure out the equivalents for many common baking ingredients. We've rounded these measurements to the nearest 5 grams to make things easier when you're measuring for a recipe. You can also find additional metric measurements on page 64.

Dried Fruits & Miscellaneous Pantry Items	Measurements						
	1/4 cup	1/3 cup	1/2 cup	2/3 cup	3/4 cup	1 cup
Almond paste	75 g	100 g	150 g	200 g	225 g	300 g
Apricots, whole, dried	45 g	60 g	90 g	120 g	135 g	180 g
Cherries, dried	35 g	45 g	70 g	90 g	105 g	140 g
Chocolate chips	45 g	60 g	90 g	120 g	135 g	180 g
Cocoa powder	20 g	25 g	40 g	50 g	60 g	80 g
Coconut oil	55 g	75 g	110 g	150 g	165 g	220 g
Cornstarch	35 g	45 g	70 g	90 g	105 g	140 g
Cranberries, dried	35 g	45 g	70 g	90 g	105 g	140 g
Currants, dried	35 g	45 g	70 g	90 g	105 g	140 g

	1/4 cup	1/3 cup	1/2 cup	2/3 cup	3/4 cup	1 cup
Flaxseed meal	25 g	30 g	45 g	60 g	75 g	90 g
Graham cracker crumbs	30 g	40 g	60 g	80 g	90 g	120 g
Jam	75 g	100 g	150 g	200 g	225 g	300 g
Nut butter	65 g	85 g	130 g	170 g	195 g	260 g
Nutella	70 g	95 g	140 g	190 g	210 g	280 g
Oats, rolled	25 g	30 g	50 g	60 g	75 g	100 g
Powdered milk	35 g	45 g	70 g	90 g	105 g	140 g
Raisins	35 g	45 g	70 g	90 g	105 g	140 g
Salt, fine sea (dry)	75 g	100 g	150 g	200 g	225 g	300 g
Salt, fine sea (moist)	50 g	65 g	100 g	130 g	150 g	200 g
Salt, kosher (Diamond)	40 g	55 g	80 g	110 g	105 g	160 g
Salt, kosher (Morton's)	60 g	80 g	120 g	160 g	180 g	240 g
Salt, table	70 g	95 g	150 g	190 g	220 g	280 g
Shortening	45 g	60 g	90 g	120 g	135 g	180 g

Sweeteners

Measurements						
	1/4 cup	1/3 cup	1/2 cup	2/3 cup	3/4 cup	1 cup
Brown sugar (packed)	50 g	65 g	100 g	130 g	150 g	200 g
Corn syrup (light)	30 g	105 g	160 g	210 g	240 g	320 g

	85 g	115 g	170 g	230 g	255 g	340 g
Honey	85 g	115 g	170 g	230 g	255 g	340 g
Molasses	80 g	105 g	160 g	210 g	240 g	320 g
Sugar, confectioners'	30 g	40 g	60 g	80 g	90 g	120 g
Sugar, granulated	50 g	65 g	100 g	130 g	150 g	200 g
Sugar, turbinado	50 g	65 g	100 g	130 g	150 g	200 g

Measurements

Nuts and Seeds	1/4 cup	1/3 cup	1/2 cup	2/3 cup	3/4 cup	1 cup
Almonds, sliced	25 g	35 g	50 g	70 g	75 g	100 g
Almonds, whole	35 g	45 g	70 g	90 g	105 g	140 g
Cashews, whole	35 g	45 g	70 g	90 g	105 g	140 g
Chia seeds	45 g	60 g	90 g	120 g	135 g	180 g
Coconut, sweetened shredded	15 g	20 g	30 g	40 g	45 g	60 g
Coconut, unsweetened shredded	20 g	25 g	40 g	50 g	60 g	80 g
Flax seeds	40 g	55 g	80 g	110 g	120 g	160 g
Hazelnuts, whole	30 g	40 g	60 g	80 g	90 g	120 g
Peanuts, whole	35 g	45 g	70 g	90 g	105 g	140 g

	1/4 cup	1/3 cup	1/2 cup	2/3 cup	3/4 cup	1 cup
Pecans, halved	30 g	40 g	60 g	80 g	90 g	120 g
Pine nuts	30 g	40 g	60 g	80 g	90 g	120 g
Pistachios, shelled whole	35 g	45 g	70 g	90 g	105 g	140 g
Poppy seeds	35 g	45 g	70 g	90 g	105 g	140 g
Pumpkin seeds (pepitas)	35 g	45 g	70 g	90 g	105 g	140 g
Sesame seeds	35 g	45 g	70 g	90 g	105 g	140 g
Walnuts, halved	30 g	40 g	60 g	80 g	90 g	120 g

Measurements

Flours

	1/4 cup	1/3 cup	1/2 cup	2/3 cup	3/4 cup	1 cup
All-purpose	35 g	45 g	70 g	90 g	105 g	140 g
Almond meal or flour	30 g	40 g	60 g	80 g	90 g	120 g
Bread	35 g	45 g	70 g	90 g	105 g	140 g
Buckwheat	35 g	45 g	70 g	90 g	105 g	140 g
Cake	30 g	40 g	60 g	80 g	90 g	120 g
Cornmeal	35 g	45 g	70 g	90 g	105 g	140 g
Oat	30 g	40 g	60 g	80 g	90 g	120 g
Pastry	35 g	45 g	70 g	90 g	105 g	140 g

	1/4 cup	1/3 cup	1/2 cup	2/3 cup	3/4 cup	1 cup
Rice	35 g	45 g	70 g	90 g	105 g	140 g
Rye	25 g	35 g	55 g	70 g	85 g	110 g
Semolina	40 g	55 g	80 g	110 g	120 g	160 g
Whole-wheat	35 g	45 g	70 g	90 g	105 g	140 g

Note: Weights were obtained using the dip-and-sweep measuring method (see page 31).

Dairy Measurements

	1/4 cup	1/3 cup	1/2 cup	2/3 cup	3/4 cup	1 cup
Butter	55 g	75 g	110 g	150 g	165 g	220 g
Cream cheese	60 g	80 g	120 g	160 g	180 g	240 g
Crème fraîche	60 g	80 g	120 g	160 g	180 g	240 g
Mascarpone	60 g	80 g	120 g	160 g	180 g	240 g
Ricotta	60 g	80 g	120 g	160 g	180 g	240 g
Sour cream	60 g	80 g	120 g	160 g	180 g	240 g
Yogurt	60 g	80 g	120 g	160 g	180 g	240 g
Yogurt, Greek	60 g	80 g	120 g	160 g	180 g	240 g

Length Equivalents

Inches	Millimeters/ centimeters
1/16	2 mm
1/8	4 mm
1/4	6 mm
1/3	8 mm
3/8	1 cm
1/2	12 mm
3/4	2 cm
1	2.5 cm

Candy Making Temperatures

Whether you're making fudge, caramel, or home-made lollipops, these are the temperatures you need to know when working with hot sugar.

- Thread (best for syrup): 223 to 234°F [106 to 112°C]

- Soft ball (best for fudge): 234 to 240°F [112 to 116°C]

- Firm ball (best for soft caramel candy): 242 to 248°F [116 to 120°C]

- Hard ball (best for nougat): 250 to 265°F [121 to 129°C]

- Soft crack (best for salt water taffy): 270 to 290°F [132 to 143°C]

- Hard crack (best for toffee): 300 to 310°F [149 to 154°C]

- Light caramel: 320 to 338°F [160 to 170°C]

- Dark caramel: 350 to 360°F [176 to 182°C]

Ingredient Substitutions

Baking powder (double-acting)
For each 1 tsp double-acting baking powder, substitute ¼ tsp baking soda and ⅝ tsp cream of tartar.

Brown sugar
For each 1 cup [200 g] packed light brown sugar, substitute 1 cup [200 g] granulated sugar and 1 Tbsp unsulfured molasses in a food processor. Pulse until the mixture is well incorporated. For dark brown sugar, increase the amount of molasses to 2 Tbsp.

Buttermilk
For each 1 cup [240 ml] buttermilk, combine 1 Tbsp fresh lemon juice with 1 cup [240 ml] whole milk and let stand for 10 minutes before using. This is known as clabbered milk.

Alternatively, combine ¾ cup [180 g] plain yogurt with ¼ cup [60 ml] milk.

Cake flour
To make the equivalent of 1 cup [120 g] cake flour, replace 2 Tbsp flour from 1 level cup [120 g] all-purpose flour with 2 Tbsp cornstarch. Sift the mixture thoroughly several times before using.

Chocolate (bittersweet)
For each 1 oz [30 g] bittersweet chocolate, substitute 2 oz [60 g] semisweet chocolate and subtract 2 Tbsp granulated sugar and 1 tsp butter, oil, or shortening from the recipe.

Chocolate (milk)
For each 1 oz [30 g] milk chocolate, substitute 1 oz [30 g] semisweet chocolate plus 1 oz [30 g] milk powder and 1 tsp granulated sugar.

Chocolate (unsweetened)

Choose one of the following as a replacement for each 1 oz [30 g] unsweetened chocolate, but keep in mind that for recipes requiring a large amount of chocolate, it's not a good idea to replace all of it with cocoa powder.

- 3 Tbsp cocoa powder plus 1 Tbsp butter, oil, or shortening.

- 2 oz [60 g] bittersweet chocolate. Subtract 2 Tbsp granulated sugar and 2 tsp butter, oil, or shortening from the recipe.

- 2 oz [60 g] semisweet chocolate. Subtract 2 Tbsp plus 2 tsp granulated sugar and 2 tsp butter, oil, or shortening from the recipe.

Cocoa powder

Cocoa powder is available in two forms: natural (often just labeled "unsweetened cocoa") and Dutch-processed. The difference in pH levels of Dutch-processed cocoa (which is neutralized with an alkaline chemical) and natural cocoa powder (which is more acidic) means they will react differently depending on the leavener in a recipe. In general, use natural cocoa powder for recipes made with alkaline leaveners like baking soda, and Dutch-processed cocoa for recipes made with baking powder, which has a neutral pH.

- For each 3 Tbsp Dutch-processed cocoa powder, substitute 3 Tbsp natural cocoa powder plus 1/8 tsp baking soda.

- For each 3 Tbsp natural cocoa powder, substitute 3 Tbsp Dutch-processed cocoa plus 1/8 tsp cream of tartar.

Confectioners' sugar

For each 1 cup [120 g] confectioners' sugar, combine 1 cup [200 g] granulated sugar and 1 tsp cornstarch in a blender. (Do not use a food processor, as it will not achieve as fine a texture.) Blend to a powdery consistency. Sift before using. This will yield slightly more than 1 cup of powdered sugar, so measure.

Cream of tartar

For each ½ tsp cream of tartar, substitute 1 tsp fresh lemon juice.

Crème fraîche

Replace with an equal quantity of strained full-fat plain (not Greek) yogurt or sour cream.

Evaporated milk

Replace with an equal quantity of half-and-half.

Half-and-half

For each 1 cup [240 ml] half-and-half, choose one of the following substitutions:

- ½ cup [120 ml] whole milk plus ½ cup [120 ml] light cream
- ¾ cup [180 ml] whole milk plus ¼ cup [60 ml] heavy cream
- ⅔ cup [165 ml] skim or low-fat milk plus ⅓ cup [75 ml] heavy cream

Milk (whole)

For each 1 cup [240 ml] whole milk, choose one of the following substitutions:

- ½ cup [120 ml] evaporated milk plus ½ cup [120 ml] water
- ¾ cup [180 ml] half-and-half plus ¼ cup [60 ml] water

- For a dairy-free substitute: 1 cup [240 ml] almond or soy milk. Coconut milk can also be used, but it may impart an undesirable flavor. Avoid rice milk and hemp milk, which result in gummy baked goods.

Self-rising flour
For each 1 cup [140 g] self-rising flour, substitute 1 cup [140 g] all-purpose flour, 1½ tsp baking powder, and ¼ tsp salt.

Sour cream
Replace with an equal amount of full-fat Greek yogurt or crème fraîche.

Superfine sugar
For each 1 cup [200 g] superfine sugar, process 1 cup plus 2 tsp [210 g] granulated sugar in a food processor for about 30 seconds.

Vanilla bean
For 1 vanilla bean, substitute 2 to 3 tsp vanilla extract.

Yogurt (non-Greek)
For each 1 cup [240 ml] substitute an equal volume of buttermilk, or mix four parts crème fraîche to one part milk.

Egg Size and Weight

Eggs play a key role in the flavor and texture of many baked goods. Unless otherwise specified, most recipes are developed with large eggs in mind.

In accordance with U.S. Department of Agriculture (USDA) guidelines, eggs are measured by minimum weight per dozen to account for small size differences among eggs in a carton.

- Small: 18 oz [510 g] (1½ oz [40 g] per egg)
- Medium: 21 oz [595 g] (1¾ oz [50 g] per egg)
- Large: 24 oz [680 g] (2 oz [55 g] per egg)
- Extra-large: 27 oz [765 g] (2¼ oz [65 g] per egg)
- Jumbo: 30 oz [850 g] (2½ oz [70 g] per egg)

If your recipe calls for an egg or two that is one size larger or smaller than what you have on hand, the differences in volume will be rather minimal; substituting one for another will be just fine. However, if you're preparing a recipe that calls for a large number of eggs, refer to the conversion chart.

Egg Size Equivalents

Small	Medium	Large	Extra-	Jumbo
1	1	1	1	1
3	2	2	2	2
4	3	3	3	2
6	5	4	4	3
7	6	5	4	4
8	7	6	5	5
9	8	7	6	6
11	9	8	7	6
12	10	9	8	7
13	11	10	9	8
15	13	11	10	9
16	14	12	11	10

To use half of an egg, whisk the egg and white together and use half of the resulting liquid.

Best Uses for Alternative Flours

The availability of alternatives to all-purpose (refined white) flour has grown in recent years to reflect a continuing interest in gluten-free baking, low-carb lifestyles, and more healthful eating. Many whole grains, nuts, and beans can be ground into flour and each one offers a distinct texture and flavor. In addition, they vary widely in protein, starch, and fiber content as well as in absorbency.

Most work best when blended with other alternative flours or combined with all-purpose flour. When baking with gluten-free flours, adding a small amount of gums or starches—such as xantham gum, guar gum, cornstarch, potato starch, or tapioca—can be useful for replacing the gluten that normally provides structure and elasticity to baked goods.

Almond flour or almond meal
Almond flour is ground more finely than almond meal. Both have a mild, nutty flavor and are best used in pancakes, quick breads, cookies, brownies, cakes, and piecrusts. Almond meal also makes a fine replacement for bread crumbs.

Buckwheat flour
Despite its name, buckwheat does not actually contain wheat. This gluten-free flour is traditionally combined with wheat flour to make soba noodles and blini. It has a delicate texture and earthy, nutty flavor that lends itself to pasta, crêpes, pancakes, waffles, and piecrusts.

Chickpea flour

This protein- and fiber-rich flour has a prominent beanlike flavor that works well in savory applications, such as vegetarian burgers, flatbreads, pizza dough, pancakes (for example, socca), and crackers.

Coconut flour

Delicately flavored and high in fiber and protein, coconut flour reacts differently in a recipe than many other flours. Because it is very absorbent, working with it requires an adjustment to the moisture or egg content. Try adding small amounts to pancakes, quick breads, brownies, cakes, and piecrusts.

Millet flour

This finely milled flour has a buttery, cornmeal-like flavor and a soft, starchy consistency. Try it in flat-breads, pizza dough, breads, and muffins.

Oat flour

Sweet and nutty oat flour gives baked goods a hearty, whole-grain flavor. Because it is high in pro-tein, fiber, and fat, it gives baked goods a moist, ten-der texture. Oat flour works well in breads, biscuits, pancakes, muffins, scones, cookies, and cakes.

Quinoa flour

Earthy and slightly bitter, quinoa flour gives baked goods a tender, moist crumb. It can be used in breads, tortillas, crackers, pancakes, crêpes, muf-fins, cookies, and cakes.

Rice flour (brown or white)
Brown rice flour and white rice flour are two of the most commonly used flours in gluten-free baking blends, but adding too much can lend grittiness to recipes. Both can be used in a variety of baked goods, particularly breads, cakes, and cookies.

Rice flour (sweet white, a.k.a. glutinous)
Traditionally used in Japanese *mochi* (rice cakes), sweet white rice flour (also known as glutinous rice flour, despite not containing gluten) has a clean, neutral flavor that works well in many baked goods. Because it is very sticky, sweet white rice flour promotes elasticity and adds structure, but should be blended with other types of flours to avoid gummy results.

Rye flour
This whole-grain flour is best known as an ingredient in dense European-style breads, but it can be used in many other applications where a nutty, earthy flavor is desired. Because rye flour is low in gluten, it should be used in conjunction with a milder wheat flour to avoid a gummy texture. Try using it in pizza dough, cookies, piecrusts, or even brownies.

Spelt flour
Made from an heirloom grain that is an ancient relative of durum wheat, spelt flour contains less gluten than whole-wheat or all-purpose flour. This nutty flour performs well in pasta, yeasted breads, pizza dough, pancakes, waffles, quick breads, cookies, and piecrusts.

Whole-wheat flour

A ubiquitous choice that can be found right next to all-purpose flour in the supermarket baking aisle, whole-wheat flour provides a hearty, deeply wheaty flavor to baked goods. Because it is high in gluten, this whole-grain flour can, in theory, be substituted for an equal amount of all-purpose flour. However, a high percentage of whole-wheat flour in a recipe can make the texture dense or even tough.

Can I replace all-purpose flour with that?

Alternative Flour	Gluten Free	Suggested percentage for replacing all-purpose flour
Almond	✓	50 to 75%
Buckwheat	✓	20 to 50%
Chickpea	✓	20 to 25%
Coconut	✓	20 to 30%
Millet	✓	20 to 30%
Oat	✓	20%
Quinoa	✓	25 to 50%
Rice (brown or white)	✓	30%
Rice (sweet white)	✓	25 to 50%
Rye		10 to 40%
Spelt		20 to 50%
Whole-wheat		25 to 50%

Note: Flours marked as gluten-free are ones that naturally do not contain gluten, but check the label to be sure they were processed in a gluten-free facility as well.

Conversions for Alternative Sweeteners

Substituting coconut palm sugar in place of granulated? The table below gives you everything you need to substitute 1 cup of sugar in a recipe with a different sweetener.

While liquid sweeteners, such as maple syrup, can be used in place of granulated sugar, the results can vary greatly. It is usually a safer bet to swap another dry sweetener for the sugar in baking.

Alternative Sweeteners (from least sweet to sweetest)	Amount	Baking Tips
Barley malt syrup	1¼ cups [425 g]. Reduce total liquid by ¼ cup [60 ml].	Strong flavor, so best used in small quantities. Can replace an equal quantity of molasses.
Brown rice syrup	1¼ cups [375 g]. Reduce overall liquid by ¼ cup [60 ml].	Mild flavor, so can replace an equal quantity of corn syrup, honey, or maple syrup.
Coconut palm sugar	1 cup [150 g]	Results may be drier; best in fat- or moisture-rich foods, such as muffins, quick breads, cookies, and caramel. Burns more quickly than white sugar.
Molasses (unsulphured, not blackstrap)	½ cup [160 g] to ¾ cup [240 g]	Strong flavor, so best used in small quantities. Great in gingerbread, spice cakes, and steamed puddings.

Sorghum syrup	¾ cup [255 g]. Reduce overall liquid by ¼ cup [60 ml].	Can replace an equal amount of corn syrup, maple syrup, molasses, or honey.
Muscovado sugar	1 cup [225 g]	Excellent replacement for brown sugar. Great in recipes where chewy, moist, or dense texture is desired.
Golden syrup	¾ cup [265 g]. Reduce overall liquid by ¼ cup [60 ml].	Can replace an equal amount of honey or corn syrup.
Maple syrup	¾ cup [180 ml]. Reduce overall liquid by ¼ cup [60 ml].	Best in muffins, quick breads, cakes, puddings, caramels, and ice cream.
Maple sugar	¾ cup [120 g]	Excellent replacement for brown sugar.
Honey	¾ cup [255 g]. Reduce overall liquid by ¼ cup [60 ml].	Reduce oven temp by 25°F [15°C] and increase baking time.
Agave syrup	¾ cup [165 g]. Reduce overall liquid by ¼ cup [60 ml].	Reduce oven temp by 25°F [15°C] and increase baking time. Can replace an equal amount of honey or maple syrup.

High-Altitude
Baking Adjustments

At high altitudes, there is less oxygen and air pressure than at sea level. As a result, water boils at a lower temperature, which means it also evaporates more quickly in the oven. Consequently, leaveners react with more impact, sugar becomes more concentrated, and whipped eggs swell more quickly. Noticeable changes begin to occur around 3,000 ft [914 m] above sea level and become more pronounced at higher elevations.

Because there are so many factors that affect high altitude baking (moisture loss, ingredients, temperature, and bake time), one set of rules cannot account for all of these considerations. However, the following tips can be used as general guidelines:

If quick breads, muffins, or chemically leavened cakes collapse, try reducing the baking powder or baking soda by ⅛ to ¼ tsp. Increasing the oven temperature by 25°F [15°C] and decreasing the baking time by about 5 minutes may also help.

Add 1 to 2 Tbsp liquid for each 1 cup of liquid in the recipe if the dough or batter seems dry.

Reduce sugar by 1½ tsp to 2 Tbsp at an elevation of 3,000 ft [914 m] above sea level, and an additional 1½ tsp to 2 Tbsp for every 2,000 ft [610 m] beyond that.

Use extra-large eggs instead of large eggs to add moisture and structure to baked goods. Or add an extra egg or yolk.

Because whipped eggs expand more quickly, both whole eggs and egg whites should be underwhipped, and whites should not be beaten beyond the soft-peak stage.

Common Baking Terms and Techniques

Blind bake
To prebake a piecrust or tart crust before adding the filling, so the bottom crust is partially or fully baked and browned. To blind bake, line an unbaked piecrust with parchment paper or aluminum foil. Add pie weights (you can use commercially made ceramic weights, dried beans or rice, or use a second pie pan), filling the crust by two-thirds. Bake at the temperature and for the amount of time directed in the recipe. The recipe should specify if the crust needs to be partially baked (generally done for fillings that that will continue baking, such as custard or pecan pies) or fully baked (for fillings that do not require baking, such as cream pies).

Cream
To beat softened butter (or shortening) and sugar together until pale, light, and fluffy. This aerates the mixture, providing lift and fluffiness to cakes and cookies.

Crimp/flute
To pinch the border of a pastry shell or piecrust together using fingers, a fork, or a pastry crimper to create a raised, decorative edge.

Cut in
To incorporate pieces of cold, solid fat (such as butter, shortening, or lard) into a flour mixture until small particles (typically the size of peas) are formed. This can be done using two knives, a fork, fingers, a pastry cutter, or a food processor. This technique is frequently used when making pie dough, scones, and biscuits.

Dip and sweep

This technique for measuring flour provides the most accurate results when weighing ingredients is not an option. To do so, gently stir the flour to ensure it is not compacted, then scoop the flour using a dry measuring cup until it overflows. Use a knife or spatula to level the top, removing the excess flour.

Egg wash

A mixture of egg (white, yolk, or whole) beaten with water, milk, or cream, which is lightly brushed onto bread, pastries, piecrusts, and other baked goods before baking to give the surface a golden, glossy appearance. In French, it's known as *dorure*.

Fold

To use a rubber spatula to gently combine ingredients and prevent overmixing. Typically, this method is used when incorporating a light and airy mixture (such as whipped egg whites) into a heavier batter or when blending inclusions (such as chopped nuts or chocolate chips) into a dough or batter.

Glaze

A thin, shiny, liquid coating that is drizzled or brushed onto finished baked goods. Examples include a sugar glaze, chocolate coating, or melted jelly.

Knead

The process of mixing and working dough into a smooth, cohesive ball. This can be accomplished in several ways: by hand (repeatedly folding, pressing down, and turning the dough), using a food processor, or using an electric mixer fitted with a dough hook. Kneading develops the network of gluten strands in the dough, making the dough stronger and more elastic.

Packed cup
A unit of measure that is made by firmly pressing or compacting an ingredient (in baking, typically brown sugar) into a dry measuring cup.

Proof
To activate yeast by dissolving it into a warm liquid (water and a pinch of sugar, or milk) and setting it aside for 5 to 10 minutes, until foamy.

In bread baking, *proof* also refers to the final rise (also known as *secondary* or *final fermentation*), after the dough has been shaped and before it is baked. Sometimes, however, the term is used interchangeably with *fermentation*, the initial period in which the dough rests and rises before it is shaped.

Sift
To pass flour or dry ingredients through a sifter or sieve to eliminate clumps and aerate the mixture. For different sifting techniques, see page 34.

Soft peaks
Refers to the consistency of whipped egg whites (or cream) that just hold their shape and droop softly when the whisk or beater is pulled out of the bowl and turned upside down.

Stiff peaks
Refers to the consistency of whipped egg whites (or cream) that stand straight up when the whisk is pulled out of the bowl and turned upside down.

Toast (nuts, spices, or coconut)
Toasting brings out the flavor and aroma of nuts, spices, and dried coconut flakes. They can all be toasted on the stove top: Place in a dry skillet over

medium heat and cook, stirring frequently, until fragrant and lightly browned, about 1 to 2 minutes. To toast nuts or coconut flakes in the oven (toasting spices in the oven is not recommended), spread out in a single layer on a rimmed baking sheet. Place in a preheated 325 to 350°F [165 to 180°C] oven and toast until fragrant and lightly browned, 5 to 10 minutes, stirring occasionally.

Whip
To whisk or beat egg whites or cream with the purpose of aerating and increasing the volume. Recipes may specify the final volume (e.g., doubled), appearance (e.g., pale yellow), or texture (e.g., soft peaks).

Sifting Techniques

Sifting aerates (lightens) flour, eliminating clumps and making it easier to incorporate into a dough or batter. It is also used to combine dry ingredients.

Sifted flour weighs less than unsifted flour, so if a recipe calls for 2 cups [240 g] *sifted flour*, the flour is sifted before it's measured. If it calls for 2 cups [280 g] *flour, sifted*, the flour is measured and then sifted. It's important to follow the directions for the best results. There are at least three methods for sifting flours:

Handheld sifter

Place the sifter over a large bowl. Spoon the flour, and any additional dry ingredients, such as salt and a leavener, into the sifter (or dump in the flour with a measuring cup if you're measuring first). Turn the crank or squeeze the handle until all of the flour passes through the mesh grid and into the bowl.

Strainer

Hold the strainer over a large bowl and add the flour and any additional dry ingredient. Using your free hand, tap the sieve repeatedly until the flour passes through into the bowl.

Whisk

This method is best for cookies and sturdier baked goods that do not require well-aerated flour to ensure a fine crumb (angel food cake or chiffon cake, for instance). Simply whisk the flour and any additional dry ingredients in a large mixing bowl. This will break up any large clumps, but will not separate the particles as finely as using a sifter or sieve would. If the recipe calls for a certain amount of presifted flour, be sure to measure the flour before whisking—otherwise, you will end up using more than you need.

Types of Chocolate by Cocoa Percentage

When it comes to chocolate, everyone has a favorite. And when baking with chocolate, it's good to know how sweet or bitter it is to ensure that the finished product will turn out just right. While there's no substitute for just taking a bite, knowing the percentage of pure cocoa solids in a chocolate bar (which makes it taste chocolaty but also somewhat bitter) or in a bag of chips is a good way to gauge how much flavor and sweetness the chocolate will impart. For bars and bags that don't list the percentage on the outside, here's a helpful guide to help you determine what you've got:

White chocolate It has no cocoa solids, but white chocolate does have cocoa butter and some milk solids as well. It's generally the sweetest type of chocolate you can get, since it doesn't have the bitter notes that cocoa solids add.

Milk chocolate Mild in flavor, this chocolate contains at least 10 percent cocoa solids and 12 percent milk solids. It's the only type of brown chocolate that is required to have added milk, which lends sweetness.

Semisweet This chocolate contains between 15 and 35 percent cocoa solids, which make it slightly more bitter than milk chocolate, though it is still on the sweet side.

Bittersweet Also known as dark chocolate, bittersweet has more than 35 percent cocoa solids. There is no maximum percentage, so take a bite to determine how bitter or sweet a particular bar or chip is.

Unsweetened This chocolate is just what it sounds like; there is no added sugar. Because of its extremely bitter flavor, it's best to use it only in recipes that specifically call for it.

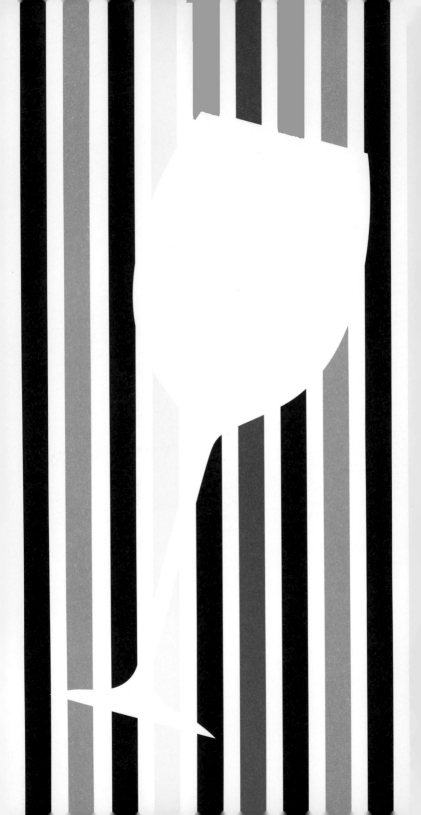

Basic Cocktail Equipment

The must-haves

shot glass (1), shaker (2), mixing glass (3), strainer (4), corkscrew (5), measuring spoons (6), bottle opener (7)

The nice-to-haves

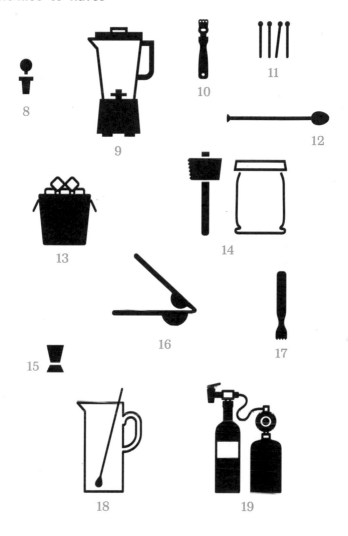

bottle stopper (8), blender (9), citrus peeler (10), cocktail picks or toothpicks (11), cocktail spoon or stirrer (12), ice bucket (13), ice mallet and bag (14), jigger and pony (15), juice squeezer (16), muddler (17), pitcher and stirrer (18), wine keeper (19)

Standard Bar Measurements

Jigger	Ounces
1	1½ [45 ml]
1½	2¼ [65 ml]
2	3 [90 ml]
Pony	1 [30 ml]
Standard shot	1 to 1½ [30 to 45 ml]
Double shot	2 to 3 [60 to 90 ml]

Note: On a bartender's double or dual jigger, the larger cup ranges from 1½ to 2 oz [45 to 65 ml], while the smaller one ranges from ¾ to 1 oz [20 to 30 ml], depending on the brand.

Serving Sizes for Alcohol

It's no surprise that beer, wine, and liquor don't all pack the same punch. When you're talking about "number of drinks," remember that the following are equivalent in terms of the amount of alcohol they contain.

One 12-oz [360-ml] beer (5 percent alcohol) = 8 to 9 oz [240 to 270 ml] malt liquor (beer above 5 percent alcohol) = 5 oz [150 ml] wine (around 12 percent alcohol) = 1½ oz [45 ml] distilled spirits (about 80 proof, 40 percent alcohol).

Liqueurs

Despite having similar spellings, liqueurs should not be confused with liquor. Liqueurs are sweetened spirits flavored with ingredients like fruit, nuts, spices, herbs, roots, bark, leaves, and seeds.

In the lists below, the liqueurs are grouped by basic flavor profiles and include generic as well as trademarked options.

Anise-flavored liqueurs
Absinthe, anesone, anisette, Herbsaint, ouzo, pastis, Pernod, sambuca

Chocolate liqueurs
Crème de cacao, Cuor di Cioccolata, Godiva

Coffee liqueurs
Capucello, crème de café, Kahlúa, Patrón XO Cafe, Tia Maria

Cream liqueurs
Amarula (marula fruit and cream), Irish cream (Irish whisky and cream), Guappa (brandy and buffalo milk)

Fruit liqueurs
Apricot: crème d'abricots
Banana: crème de banane
Black currant: crème de cassis
Cherry: crème de cerise, Cherry Heering
Honeydew melon: Midori
Lemon: limoncello
Orange: Aperol, Cointreau, Blue Curaçao, Grand Marnier, Triple Sec

Passion fruit: Alizé Gold Passion
Peach and citrus: Southern Comfort
Pineapple: crème d'ananas
Raspberry: Chambord, framboise
Sloe plum: sloe gin

Herb and flower liqueurs
Cinnamon: Goldschlager, Goldwasser
(cinnamon, anise, black licorice, orange)
Elderflower: St-Germain
Herbs: Galliano, Jägermeister, Drambuie (herbs
and honey), Bénédictine (herbs, fruit peels, citrus,
honey), Chartreuse (herbs, spices, flowers)
Mint: crème de menthe, Friesengeist
Rose: crème de rose
Violet: crème de violette

Nut liqueurs
Almond: amaretto, crème d'amande,
crème de noyaux
Hazelnut: Frangelico
Walnut: nocino (green walnut), Nocello
(walnut and hazelnut)

Cocktail Garnishes

A garnish is sometimes an essential component of a cocktail, sometimes it adds an accent flavor or fragrance that makes the drink unique, and sometimes it's there mostly for looks (and there's nothing wrong with that!). In a well-stocked kitchen, there are plenty of options for garnishes that complement the cocktails you're crafting—from fresh fruits and vegetables, to herbs and spices, to pantry staples such as salt, sugar, and olives.

Salted or sugared rim

A salted rim is classic for a margarita and a sugared rim is standard on a brandy crusta, but these embellishments can also be used on other cocktails. To salt or sugar the rim of a glass, first place the salt or sugar in a shallow dish with a diameter that is larger than the mouth of the glass. Moisten the rim of the empty glass by running a wedge of citrus around it, or by dipping it into a saucer of water. Invert the glass into the salt or sugar to coat the rim. If convenient, glasses can be salted or sugared several hours in advance and allowed to dry, which sets (hardens) the salt or sugar.

For salted rims, use coarse, flaky salt like kosher salt. For sugared rims, both granulated and superfine sugars work well. For added flavor and visual interest, you can mix other ingredients, such as spices and seasonings, into the salt or sugar. Here are some ideas:

• cayenne

• chili powder

• cocoa powder

- finely grated citrus zest

- ground black pepper

- ground cardamom

- ground cinnamon

- smoked paprika

Rim of the glass garnishes

Some ingredients are meant to perch on the glass, rather than sit in the drink itself. It can be a nice way to add some decoration, and in some cases it gives your guest the choice whether to add a strong flavor to the drink or keep it on the side. Here are some ideas:

- citrus spiral

- citrus wheel or half wheel

- citrus wedge

- cucumber wheel

- jalapeño slice

- star anise

Garnishes to add to the glass

A garnish added to the cocktail, either sitting in the glass or dusted over the top, can add both flavor and aroma to a drink. Be sure to choose one that complements your cocktail since even if you fish it out, the flavor will remain. Here are some ideas:

- basil

- celery stick

- cinnamon stick

- citrus twist

- citrus wedge

- cocktail onions

- cucumber spears

- grape tomatoes

- grated nutmeg

- lavender

- lemongrass

- long-stemmed caper berry

- mint

- olives

- pickled green beans

- rosemary

- thyme

Cocktail pick garnishes

Items skewered on cocktail picks are easy embellishments, and give guests the choice of adding the flavor to their drink or keeping it separate. Use just one or stack and skewer multiples, depending on what's appropriate for the drink. Avoid using ingredients that are too soft to stay on the pick (for example, ripe mango) and those that discolor (for example, apples). Here are some ideas:

- cocktail onions

- dragonfruit chunks

- fresh berries

- fresh fig wedges or rounds

- grape tomatoes

- jalapeño (cut into thick slices)

- kiwi chunks

- kumquats

- Luxardo or maraschino cherries

- melon chunks or balls

- olives

- pickled green beans (cut into sections)

- pineapple chunks or wedges

- rosemary (use it as the skewer)

- seedless grapes

Ice cube garnishes
If you're the type who plans in advance and if appropriate for the cocktails you're serving, try freezing ingredients into ice cubes. The ice does double duty: it keeps the drink cold *and* serves as a garnish. Drop the ingredient of choice into an ice cube tray, fill the tray with water, and freeze. Combine ingredients—for example, mint with raspberry—for a striking visual. Here are some ideas:

- citrus cut into small pieces

- edible flowers

- fresh berries

- fresh herbs

- kiwi chunks

- melon balls

- pomegranate seeds

- seedless grapes

Glassware Glossary

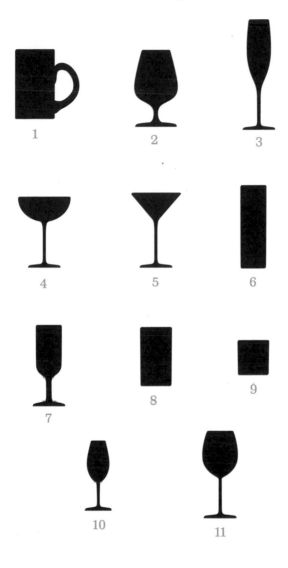

beer mug (1) , brandy snifter (2), Champagne flute (3), Champagne coupe (4), cocktail glass (5), collins glass (6), cordial glass (7), highball glass (8), old-fashioned glass (9), sherry or port glass (10), wineglass (11)

Wines

The following tables provide relevant information for popular white, red, and sparkling wines. The sparkling wines are listed alphabetically, while the non-sparkling white and red wines are listed according to their grape varietal, beginning with light-bodied wines and ending with full-bodied ones. Bear in mind that the world of wine is vast, and even wines made from the same grape can differ in body and flavor, depending on where the grapes were grown and how the wine was produced. So notes about flavor profile are general, and there are exceptions. Use the information below as a starting point to learn more about the world of wine, and then form your own opinions.

White Wine Grapes

Grape Varietal	Flavor Profile
Albariño or Alvarinho (Spanish)	Light bodied, high in acidity, with flavors of citrus, melon, pineapple, and peach or apricot
Vermentino (Italian)	Light to medium bodied with bright acidity; complex and fruity flavor, with notes of grapefruit, apple, and tropical fruit; a good alternative to Sauvignon Blanc
Riesling (German)	Light to medium bodied with excellent acidity; exhibits floral and mineral notes and flavors of ripe peach, apricot, apple, and pear
Pinot Gris (French) or Pinot Grigio (Italian)	Light to medium bodied with moderate acidity; primary flavors include lemon, apple, melon, and stone fruit; Italian varieties are minerally and dry, while the French style is more fruity and honeylike

Grüner Veltliner (Austrian)	Light to medium bodied with high acidity; flavors range from lemon, lime, and apple to honey, nuts, and white pepper, depending on the style (light and zesty or rich and peppery)
Chenin Blanc (French, South Africa)	Light to medium bodied with striking acidity; fruit flavors range from apple and pear to citrus, with honey and floral aromas; late-harvest version is sweet
Torrontés (Argentinan)	Medium-light bodied with medium acidity; exhibits flavors of citrus, pear, and peach, with grassy and floral notes
Pinot Blanc (French) or Pinot Bianco (Italian)	Medium-light to medium bodied with moderate acidity; flavors of apple and citrus, with honey and almond notes; often compared to Chardonnay, but is generally less complex
Sauvignon Blanc (French)	Medium-light to medium bodied and crisp, with noticeable acidity; herbaceous, flavors of green fruit, with flinty undertones
Gewürztraminer (German)	Medium bodied, low acidity, and fruit forward, with heady aromas of roses, lychee, and warm spices; relatively high alcohol content; available in dry, off-dry, and late-harvest dessert wine styles
Viognier (French)	Medium to full bodied, with moderate acidity; extremely fragrant, with aromas of peach, apricot, honeysuckle, and tangerine; often blended with other whites or with Syrah
Chardonnay (French)	Full bodied, medium acidity, with notes of apple, lemon, melon, pineapple, and vanilla; buttery and creamy when oaked

Red Wine Grapes

Grape Varietal	Flavor Profile
Gamay	Light bodied, fruity, flowery, with hints of earthiness and a pleasing acidity; used to make Beaujolais; good and less expensive alternative to Pinot Noir
Pinot Noir (French)	Light to medium bodied with notable acidity and complex notes of cherry, raspberry, spice, and earth
Sangiovese (Italian)	Wide variation with this varietal—body ranges from light-medium to medium-full; flavors range from simple and fruity to rich, leathery, and minerally; the base of Chianti wines
Cabernet Franc (French)	Medium bodied, subtly fruity and spicy, with green bell pepper and other vegetal notes; part of the Bordeaux blend
Grenache (French) or Garnacha (Spanish)	Medium bodied with a flavor profile that varies, based on where the grapes are grown, but typically includes red berries, cherries, citrus zest, spices, and tobacco
Barbera (Italian)	Medium bodied but with deep coloring and high acidity, flavor notes of cherry and blackberry, along with hints of spice and smoke; good alternative to Chianti
Merlot (French)	Medium to medium-full bodied and silky, with flavors of dark cherries, black plums, blackberries, and sometimes chocolate and tobacco, depending on the growing region

Montepulciano (Italian)	Medium–full bodied with ample acidity, flavors of dark plum and sour cherry, with hints of cocoa and herbs
Tempranillo (Spain)	Medium–full bodied with notes of dark cherry and leather; tomato and herb nuances lend a savory quality; a good alternative to more expensive Cabernet Sauvignon
Nebbiolo (Italian)	Full bodied with high acidity and an aroma of roses and fruit; flavor notes of cherry, leather, and licorice, and sometimes touches of dried fruit and herbs
Malbec (French, Argentinian)	Full bodied, with a flavor profile that varies—Argentinian Malbec features plump, ripe, dark fruits with hints of chocolate and tobacco; French Malbec tends toward savory with notes of black pepper and leather; good and inexpensive alternative to Syrah and Cabernet Sauvignon
Zinfandel (French)	Full bodied, with notable sweetness and acidity and flavors of ripe raspberry, blackberry, and dark plums, and a finish of subtle spice and tobacco; higher alcohol than most wines
Cabernet Sauvignon (French)	Full bodied, with a complex flavor profile that includes dark cherry and blackberry and hints of vanilla, as well as savory notes of olives and green bell pepper; part of the Bordeaux blend
Syrah (French) or Shiraz (Australian)	Very full bodied, jammy, with flavors of ripe dark berries and notes of chocolate, black pepper, and smoke

Petite Sirah (French, Californian)	Very full bodied, inky, and intense, with a flavor profile of ripe blueberry and blackberry, black pepper, and licorice, often with notes of vanilla and chocolate

Sparkling Wines

Wine	Flavor Profile
Asti Spumante (Italian)	Light, fresh, and effervescent, with perfumed notes of peach, pear, orange, and apricot
Cava (Spanish)	Depending on aging and quality, flavor notes range from crisp and fruity to toasty with savory notes; typically dry but made in a range of styles, from brut nature (driest) to dulce (sweetest)
Champagne (French)	Citrus and stone-fruit flavors dominate, with nutty and toasty aromas developing with age; typically dry but available in a range of styles, from extra brut (very dry) to doux (very sweet)
Lambrusco (Italian)	Fruity and sometimes floral; made in different styles: secco (dry), semisecco (off-dry), amabile (lightly sweet), and dolce (sweet)
Prosecco (Italian)	Fresh and fruity, with flavors of apple, pear, and peach, combined with floral aromas
Sekt (German and Austrian)	Generally sweeter and lower in alcohol than most other sparkling wines; typically fruity but flavor can vary widely depending on varietals used

Beer Styles Glossary

Demystify the beer section of a menu with this handy little glossary of the most common beer styles, organized from light to dark:

Lager
A refreshing cold-brewed style of beer that can be bubbly, light, and relatively neutral in flavor.

Kolsch
A German beer that tends to be dry and crisp in flavor, occasionally with notes of bitterness, depending on the recipe.

Pilsner
Czech in origin, this golden beer tends to have medium to strong notes of citrus and bitterness.

Tripel
A type of Belgian beer that can be lightly floral, fruity, and creamy, which often masks its typically high alcohol content.

Sour
Fermented with wine yeast, this unique beer tends to mimic a dry white wine with punches of sour and floral notes.

Pale ale
Often with light notes of bitterness, this style can have pungent floral or citrusy notes.

IPA
A favorite of hops lovers, this style ranges in bitterness and astringency, depending on the recipe.

Amber ale
An ideal introduction to craft beer. Most ambers tend to balance perfectly between a malty and bitter profile.

Red ale
Typically malt–forward, this medium to dark beer can be sweet and biscuitlike in taste.

Bock
A dark springtime beer, this style tends to be lightly hopped with a smooth, toasted finish.

Brown ale
A versatile, malty beer that can range from sweet to bitter, depending on the brewer.

Porter
The use of roasted malt often gives this dark beer a warm, smooth character; it can have mild notes of burnt sweetness (think caramel or toffee) or slight hints of bitter.

Stout
This robust, deeply colored style is a coffee-lover's kind of beer with a creamy, bitter, dark chocolate character.

Coffee Drinks

No longer will you have to stare at the list of drinks at a coffee shop and wonder what exactly you're getting. And an added bonus: you'll also be able to re-create them at home.

Affogato Espresso poured over ice cream (1).

Americano Espresso shot with hot water added (2).

Café au lait Equal parts drip coffee and steamed milk (3).

Café cubano Espresso shot sweetened with sugar as it is brewed (4).

Cappuccino Espresso with steamed milk, topped with foam (5).

Cold brew Coarsely ground coffee brewed in room temperature water for an extended period of time (6).

Cortado Equal parts espresso and steamed milk (7).

Espresso Coffee brewed by forcing a small amount of boiling water under pressure through finely ground beans (8).

Iced coffee Pour over coffee that is left to cool to room temperature and poured over ice, or that is brewed with less water and poured over ice while still hot (9).

Latte (sometimes called a flat white) Espresso with steamed milk and little or no foam (10).

Machiatto Espresso shot with a small amount of foamed milk (11).

Mocha Espresso with steamed milk and chocolate—either melted chocolate or chocolate syrup (12).

Pour over Coffee brewed by pouring just-boiled water over and through grounds, generally coarsely ground (13).

Red eye Pour over coffee with a shot of espresso (14).

Turkish coffee Coffee brewed by simmering fine grounds in water, sometimes with sugar. The finished coffee is not filtered, so the grounds should settle before drinking (15).

Types of Tea

Most tea comes from the same plant, *Camellia sinensis*. It's the way it's processed that makes the biggest difference in flavor. Here's a breakdown of different types of tea, from lightest to darkest, with a few popular nonteas as well.

White Traditionally white tea is made from the leaves of the youngest new shoots of a tea plant. The leaves are allowed to wither fully and dry at a cool temperature, generally without humidity. It should be brewed in water around 190°F [90°C].

Green Green tea is made from tea leaves that are slightly withered in a humid environment after picking to allow partial oxidation, and then dried in high heat for a short period of time. It should be brewed in water between 175 and 185°F [80 to 85°C].

Matcha Made from the finely ground powder of green tea leaves that are shaded from direct sunlight during the last few weeks of their growth, which turns the leaves a darker green. Matcha is graded; higher grades have a better color and flavor.

Oolong Somewhere between a green and black tea, oolong is made from leaves that are more oxidized than green tea, but not as fully oxidized as black. The tea leaves are allowed to sit in humid environments until the leaves darken; they are sometimes rolled or twisted to encourage further oxidation. There is not a lot of uniformity among oolong teas, so examine or taste the tea before buying. If it is a lighter shade, brew it as you would green tea. If it is darker, brew it more like black tea.

Black Black tea is made from tea leaves that are left to fully oxidize and wither in a hot, humid environment before being dried. in some cases, the leaves are roasted, twisted, or rolled to encourage further oxidation before drying. Brew black tea in water that is between 200 and 212°F [95 to 100°C].

Pu'er Aged black tea, most common in China. This tea is fully oxidized and fermented before it is dried; has a deep, almost peaty flavor; and little to no bitterness. It should be brewed in water that is between 200 and 212°F [95 to 100°C].

Chai Chai is not really a tea, but rather a mix of spices that are steeped in hot water to create a tealike beverage. Recipes vary widely, but many chai mixes include cinnamon, clove, ginger, and black peppercorns, and some also include tea—either black, green, or rooibos. Chai is often steeped in hot milk, or a mix of milk and water. If it contains tea, brew it at the temperature recommended for that tea. Otherwise, brew it in water or milk that is just under boiling, around 205°F [95°C].

Roiboos Native to South Africa, rooibos is the leaf of a reddish-brown plant (*roiboos* is the Afrikaans word for "red bush"). Like other tea leaves, the level of oxidation determines the color. More oxidized leaves turn red, and those are the most common variety of this tea worldwide. It should be brewed in water around 200 to 212°F [95 to 100°C].

Basic Cooking Equipment

The must-haves

9-x-13-in [23-x-33-cm] baking dish (1), box grater (2), colander or large strainer (3), cutting boards (at least three) (4), set of knives (paring, long serrated (for bread), chef's) (5), 9-in [23-cm] skillet (nonstick or stainless) (6), peeler (7), 3-qt [2.8-L] saucepan with lid (8), sheet pan with rack (9), metal spatula (10), stockpot with lid (11), meat thermometer (12), tongs (13), wooden spoons (14), measuring cups and spoons (15)

The nice-to-haves

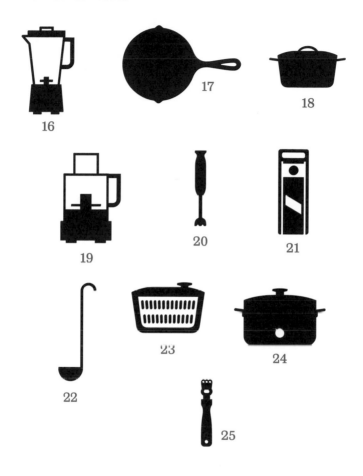

blender (16), 12-in [30-cm] cast-iron skillet (17), 5-qt [4.7-L] Dutch oven (18), food processor (19), immersion blender (20), mandolin (21), ladle (22), salad spinner (23), slow cooker (24), zester (25)

Metric Conversions for Beans, Grains, Produce, Cheese

If you prefer to weigh your ingredients in grams, but your recipes list them in cups, or vice versa, this handy chart will help you figure out the equivalents for many basic ingredients. We've rounded these measurements to the nearest 5 grams to make things easier when you're measuring for a recipe. You can also find additional metric measurements on page 12.

Dry Grains	Cups and Grams							
	1 Tbsp	1/4 cup	1/3 cup	1/2 cup	2/3 cup	3/4 cup	1 cup
Amaranth	10 g	45 g	60 g	90 g	120 g	135 g	180 g
Barley	10 g	50 g	65 g	100 g	130 g	150 g	200 g
Buckwheat groats	10 g	45 g	60 g	90 g	120 g	135 g	180 g
Bulgur	10 g	40 g	55 g	80 g	110 g	120 g	160 g
Couscous	10 g	45 g	60 g	90 g	120 g	135 g	180 g
Couscous, Israeli	10 g	35 g	45 g	70 g	90 g	105 g	140 g
Farro	10 g	45 g	60 g	90 g	120 g	135 g	180 g
Grits	10 g	35 g	45 g	70 g	90 g	105 g	160 g
Kasha	10 g	45 g	60 g	90 g	120 g	135 g	180 g
Millet	10 g	45 g	60 g	90 g	120 g	135 g	180 g

Oats, rolled	5 g	25 g	30 g	50 g	60 g	75 g	100 g
Amaranth oats, steel-cut	10 g	40 g	55 g	80 g	110 g	120 g	160 g
Polenta	10 g	35 g	45 g	70 g	90 g	105 g	140 g
Popcorn (unpopped)	15 g	50 g	65 g	100 g	130 g	150 g	200 g
Quinoa	10 g	45 g	60 g	90 g	120 g	135 g	180 g
Rice, medium-grain	15 g	50 g	65 g	100 g	130 g	150 g	200 g
Rice, long-grain	15 g	50 g	65 g	100 g	130 g	150 g	200 g
Rice, short-grain	15 g	50 g	65 g	100 g	130 g	150 g	200 g
Rice, wild	10 g	45 g	60 g	90 g	120 g	135 g	180 g
Wheat germ	5 g	20 g	25 g	40 g	50 g	60 g	80 g

Cups and Grams

Beans and Pulses	3 Tbsp	1/4 cup	1/3 cup	1/2 cup	2/3 cup	3/4 cup	1 cup
Black beans, dried	35 g	45 g	60 g	90 g	120 g	135 g	180 g
Cannellini, dried	30 g	40 g	55 g	80 g	110 g	120 g	160 g
Chickpeas, dried	35 g	45 g	60 g	90 g	120 g	135 g	180 g
Kidney beans, dried	30 g	40 g	55 g	80 g	110 g	120 g	160 g
Lentils, brown	40 g	50 g	65 g	100 g	130 g	150 g	200 g

	1 Tbsp	3 Tbsp	1/4 cup	1/3 cup	1/2 cup	2/3 cup	3/4 cup	1 cup
Lentils, green (du Puy)								
	40g	50 g	65 g	100 g	130 g	150 g	200 g	
Lentils, red	40g	50 g	65 g	100 g	130 g	150 g	200 g
Pinto beans, dried	35g	45 g	60 g	90 g	120 g	135 g	180 g
Split peas	40 g	50 g	65 g	100 g	130 g	150 g	200 g

Vegetables

Cups and Grams

	1 Tbsp	3 Tbsp	1/4 cup	1/3 cup	1/2 cup	2/3 cup	3/4 cup	1 cup
Arugula, baby (packed leaves)			5 g	7 g	10 g	13 g	15 g	20 g
Cabbage, shredded			15 g	20 g	30 g	40 g	50 g	60 g
Carrot, fine dice			35 g	45 g	70 g	90 g	105 g	140 g
Carrot, medium dice			35 g	45 g	70 g	90 g	105 g	140 g
Celery, fine dice	10 g	25 g	30 g	40 g	60 g	80 g	90 g	120 g
Celery, medium dice	10 g	25 g	30 g	40 g	60 g	80 g	90 g	120 g
Corn kernels, fresh, cooked (cut off the cobs)	10 g	30 g	40 g	55 g	80 g	110 g	120 g	160 g
Corn kernels, raw (frozen and fresh)			35 g	45 g	70 g	90 g	105 g	140 g
Fennel, diced			25 g	35 g	50 g	70 g	75 g	100 g
Green onions, sliced	3 g	9 g	12 g	16 g	24 g	32 g	36 g	48 g

	1 Tbsp	3 Tbsp	1/4 cup	1/3 cup	1/2 cup	2/3 cup	3/4 cup	1 cup
Kale, roughly chopped								15 g
Leeks, diced	10 g	30 g	25 g	35 g	50 g	70 g	75 g	100 g
Lima beans, frozen			35 g	45 g	70 g	90 g	105 g	140 g
Mushrooms (white, cremini), sliced			15 g	20 g	30 g	40 g	45 g	60 g
Onion, fine dice	10 g	25 g	35 g	45 g	70 g	90 g	105 g	140 g
Onion, medium dice	10 g	25 g	35 g	45 g	70 g	90 g	105 g	140 g
Peas, frozen	10 g	25 g	30 g	40 g	60 g	80 g	90 g	120 g
Peppers (bell), fine dice			30 g	40 g	60 g	80 g	90 g	120 g
Peppers (bell), medium dice			30 g	40 g	60 g	80 g	90 g	120 g
Spinach, baby (packed leaves)			5 g	7 g	10 g	13 g	15 g	20 g
Tomatoes, grape			40 g	55 g	80 g	110 g	120 g	160 g

Herbs

Cups and Grams

	1 Tbsp	3 Tbsp	1/4 cup	1/3 cup	1/2 cup	2/3 cup	3/4 cup	1 cup
Basil, chopped	3 g	8 g	10 g	15 g	20 g	25 g	30 g	40 g
Basil, packed leaves			3 g	4 g	6 g	8 g	9 g	12 g
Cilantro, chopped	3 g	8 g	10 g	15 g	20 g	25 g	30 g	40 g
Cilantro, packed leaves			3 g	4 g	6 g	8 g	9 g	12 g

	1 Tbsp	3 Tbsp	1/4 cup	1/3 cup	1/2 cup	2/3 cup	3/4 cup	1 cup
Cilantro, tightly packed leaves			5 g	7 g	10 g	13 g	15 g	20 g
Mint, chopped			10 g	15 g	20 g	25 g	30 g	40 g
Mint, packed leaves			3 g	4 g	6 g	8 g	9 g	12 g
Parsley, chopped	3 g	8 g	10 g	15 g	20 g	25 g	30 g	40 g
Parsley, packed leaves			3 g	4 g	6 g	8 g	9 g	12 g

Dairy and Cheese

Cups and Grams

	1 Tbsp	3 Tbsp	1/4 cup	1/3 cup	1/2 cup	2/3 cup	3/4 cup	1 cup
Mayonnaise	15 g	45 g	60 g	80 g	120 g	160 g	180 g	240 g
Blue cheese, crumbled			30 g	40 g	60 g	80 g	90 g	120 g
Cheddar, grated	5 g	15 g	20 g	25 g	40 g	50 g	60 g	80 g
Feta, crumbled			30 g	40 g	60 g	80 g	90 g	120 g
Fontina, grated			20 g	25 g	40 g	50 g	60 g	80 g
Gouda, grated			20 g	25 g	40 g	50 g	60 g	80 g
Mozzarella, grated	5 g	15 g	20 g	25 g	40 g	50 g	60 g	80 g
Parmigiano, finely grated, lightly packed	2 g	6 g	8 g	10 g	15 g	20 g	25 g	30 g
Pecorino, finely grated, lightly packed	5 g	10 g	15 g	20 g	30 g	40 g	45 g	60 g

About Seasoning—
Herbs, Spices, and Salt

Freshness Is Key
Spices and dried herbs don't spoil or "go bad," but over time but they do lose their potency. Whole spices stay fresh for up to two years; ground spices and dried herbs will remain fresh for about one year. To check an opened spice or herb container, have a whiff. If its fragrance is weak or has vanished altogether, it's time to replace it. To avoid having spices and dried herbs go stale, purchase them in small quantities from a bulk bin so that you use them up and replenish them more frequently. Store in airtight jars or containers in a cool, dark spot in the pantry.

Substituting Dried Herbs for Fresh
In general, the flavor profile of dried herbs, in both taste and aroma, is very different from that of their fresh counterparts, and in many applications, they're a poor substitute. Oregano, sage, and mint generally can't be substituted dry for fresh. But, on the other hand, dried thyme and dried bay leaves are perfectly acceptable in most recipes calling for fresh.

The longer cooking the dish, the more likely that dried herbs will substitute well for the fresh stuff. If the herbs won't be cooked, like in vinaigrette, or will be added at the end of cooking, it's best to use what the recipe calls for. The general guideline when substituting dried herbs for fresh is to use one-third to one-half the amount called for, as dried herbs have a more concentrated flavor. With the exception of bay leaves, before using, it's a good idea to crumble the dried herb between your fingers to release its flavor and fragrance.

Toasting Spices
See page 32 for details on how to toast spices.

Salting Food
There are a huge variety of salts on the market, and they aren't all equivalent. For seasoning during cooking, reach for one with relatively small, evenly-shaped crystals like kosher salt, fleur de sel, or fine sea salt. If you're dressing raw foods, something with a more uneven grain can add texture, like Maldon or another kind of flaky sea salt that has relatively thin flakes. And for hearty, cooked foods, choose something with large crystals. Sel gris, or gray salt, is a coarse sea salt that won't entirely melt on hot food and adds a pleasant crunch. Mineral-rich salts, like Himalayan salt or Hawaiian sea salt, may add a light flavor that is hard to pick out, while smoked salt and seasoned blends that may include ingredients like lemon or rosemary add a noticeable taste to the final dish.

Basic Knife Techniques and Terminology

Mastery of basic knife skills will lessen your time spent at the cutting board. Keep in mind that sharp knives cut through foods more easily and make knife-prep tasks much easier and more enjoyable.

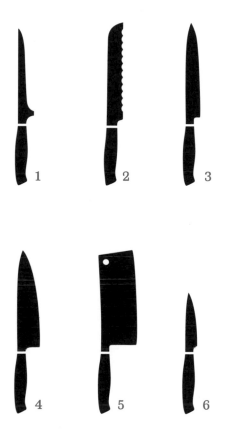

boning knife (1), bread knife (2), carving knife (3), chef's knife (4), cleaver (5), paring knife (6)

Types of Cuts

Chiffonade

To cut into ribbonlike shreds. This technique is used with broad-leaf ingredients, such as lettuce, spinach, and basil. To chiffonade, stack a few leaves on top of each other and roll into a cylinder. Use a sharp chef's knife to thinly slice the cylinder, and then fluff and separate the shreds.

Chop

To use repeated cuts with a knife to break foods down into pieces. Recipes sometimes specify the size of the pieces by stating coarsely or roughly chopped, medium chop, or finely chopped. Though there is no size standardization, "coarsely chopped" often means cut into pieces about ¾ in [2 cm], "medium chop" about ½ in [12 mm], and "finely chopped" between ¼ in [6 mm] and ⅛ in [4 mm].

Cut on the bias

To cut food on an angle. Long, slender ingredients, such as green onions, are cut on the bias by positioning the knife at roughly a 45-degree angle to the food, producing elongated slices. Meats are sliced on the bias by holding the knife so that the blade meets the surface of the food at about a 45-degree angle, producing slices with greater surface area than if the knife were held straight.

Dice

To cut food into cubes. Some recipes specify an exact size for the cubes; others may simply call for a large, medium, small, or fine dice. There is no rule, but in general, large dice are about ¾ in [2 cm], medium about ½ in [12 mm], small about ¼ in [6 mm], and fine about ⅛ in [4 mm]. (Fine dice are called brunoise in classic French cooking.)

Mince
To chop very finely. Garlic, herbs, and other ingredients that are added for flavor rather than texture or appearance are often minced.

Julienne
To cut into long, thin strips that resemble matchsticks.

Suprême
To remove the peel, pith, and membranes from a segment of citrus. To do this, use a sharp paring knife to slice off the bottom and top of the citrus and set the fruit on one of the cut ends. Working from top to bottom and following the contour of the fruit, cut away all of the peel and pith (the inner white layer). Hold the fruit in your nondominant hand and slide the knife blade along each side of the segment, inside the inner white layer, to free it from the fruit. Then repeat until all the segments have been cut out.

A Guide to Cooking Common Cuts of Meat

In this section, you'll find illustrated guides to the cuts of pork, beef, and lamb commonly found in the grocery store, with the best cooking methods listed for each cut.

Pork

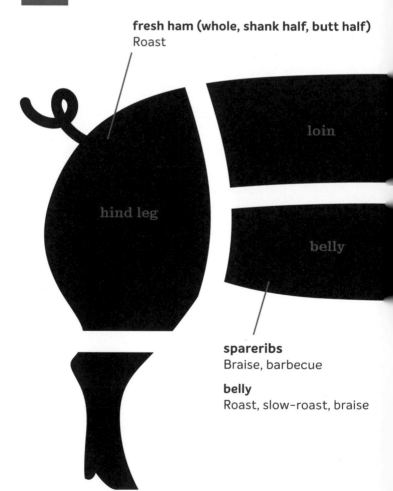

fresh ham (whole, shank half, butt half)
Roast

loin

hind leg

belly

spareribs
Braise, barbecue

belly
Roast, slow-roast, braise

loin roast (bone-in, boneless) Roast

pork chop (bone-in, boneless) Pan-sear, fry, grill

tenderloin Roast, grill, stir-fry (cut into pieces)

baby back ribs Slow-roast, barbecue

country-style ribs Braise

Boston butt
Slow-roast, barbecue, braise

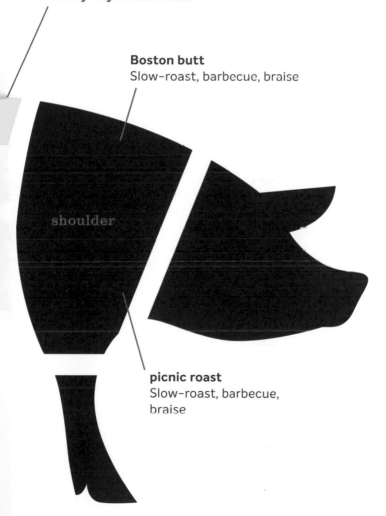

shoulder

picnic roast
Slow-roast, barbecue,
braise

Beef

strip loin roast Roast

strip steak (a.k.a. New York strip steak) Pan-sear, grill

T-bone steak Pan-sear, grill

porterhouse steak Pan-sear, grill

tenderloin (whole) Roast

tenderloin steak (a.k.a. fillet mignon) Panfry, grill

sirloin steak Pan-sear, grill

tri-tip roast Roast, grill

rump roast
Roast

top round steak
Pan-sear, grill

bottom round steak
Pan-sear, grill

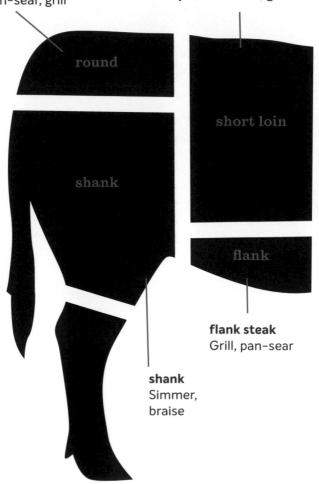

round

short loin

shank

flank

flank steak
Grill, pan-sear

shank
Simmer,
braise

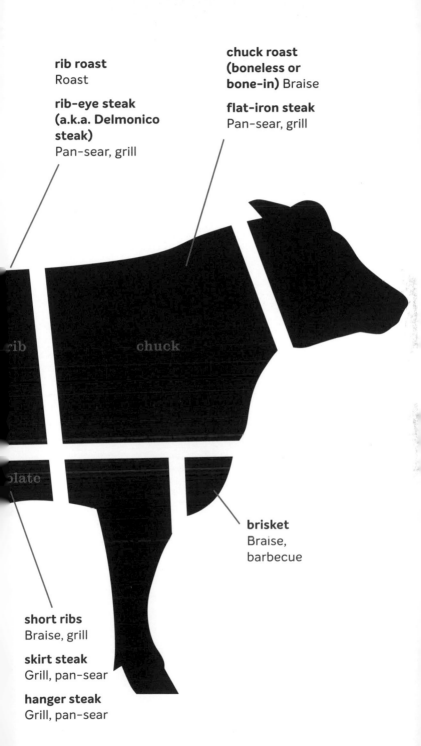

rib roast
Roast

rib-eye steak (a.k.a. Delmonico steak)
Pan-sear, grill

chuck roast (boneless or bone-in) Braise

flat-iron steak
Pan-sear, grill

rib

chuck

plate

brisket
Braise, barbecue

short ribs
Braise, grill

skirt steak
Grill, pan-sear

hanger steak
Grill, pan-sear

Lamb

leg (bone-in)
Roast

leg (boneless)
Roast, grill

loin chops
Panfry, grill

leg

loin

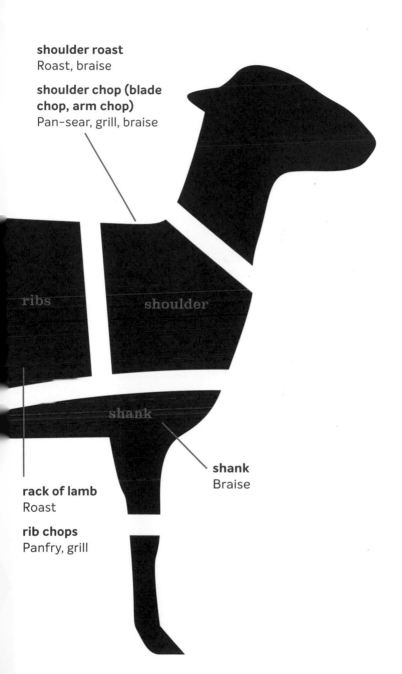

shoulder roast
Roast, braise

shoulder chop (blade chop, arm chop)
Pan-sear, grill, braise

ribs

shoulder

shank

shank
Braise

rack of lamb
Roast

rib chops
Panfry, grill

Meat Doneness Temperatures

With a meat thermometer handy, you need never worry about overcooking meat, poultry, and fish again. No matter what you're cooking, you can find both the USDA and the chef guidelines for what temperature to look for so you get the perfect doneness every time. Keep in mind that when cooking meat or fish, you should pull it out at the temperature noted below and then let it rest for about 5 minutes before carving or serving. As the meat rests, it will cook a little more, and the temperature will go up a few degrees, The resting time will allow the juices to redistribute, so they don't run out when you carve.

Beef, pork, veal, and lamb (Steaks, chops, and roasts)
USDA recommendation for minimum temperature: 145°F [63°C]

CHEF GUIDELINES:
Beef, veal, and lamb: 125 to 130°F [52 to 54°C] for rare, 130 to 140°F [54 to 60°C] for medium-rare, 140 to 150°F [60 to 66°C] for medium, 150 to 155°F [66 to 68°C] for medium-well, 155 to 160°F [68 to 71°C] for well-done

Pork: for each level of doneness, generally aim for the higher end of the above temperature spectrums.

Ground meats
USDA recommendation: 160°F [71°C]

CHEF GUIDELINES: For burgers, follow the meat doneness recommendations for steaks, chops, and roasts to cook your burger to your desired temperature.

Ham, fresh or smoked (uncooked)
USDA recommendation: 145°F [63°C]

All poultry
USDA recommendation: 165°F [74°C]

CHEF GUIDELINES: Poultry is done at around 145 to 150°F [63 to 66°C] for white meat and 155 to 160°F [68 to 71°C] for dark meat. If you're roasting a whole chicken, check both the white and dark meat for doneness and wait until both are fully cooked before taking the chicken out of the oven.

Fish and Shellfish
USDA recommendation: 145°F [63°C]

CHEF GUIDELINES: 125 to 130°F [52 to 54°C] for medium-rare, 130 to 140°F [54 to 60°C] for medium, 140 to 145°F [60 to 63°C] for well done. Also look for the fish or shellfish to become completely opaque, both outside and inside. For whitefish, look for fish that flakes easily when you gently put a fork in it and twist.

Common Cooking Terms

Here are some common cooking terms and their definitions to help you navigate your way through recipes that assume a certain level of knowledge on the part of the cook. (For knife techniques, see page 71.)

Al dente The literal meaning of this Italian term is "to the tooth," or less literally, "firm to the bite." It is often used as a doneness cue for pasta and other foods, such as the rice in risotto. Al dente foods should be mostly tender, with just a bit of resistance at the very center.

Blanch To drop foods, usually fruits or vegetables, into boiling water, leave them there for a brief time, and then remove them before they are fully cooked. Blanching is usually done to set color, loosen skin, or partially cook.

Braise/Stew To cook foods, usually proteins but sometimes vegetables, partially submerged in simmering liquid in a covered pot or pan until tender. The cooking liquid typically becomes the sauce for the dish.

Confit Food that has been slowly cooked in fat and stored in the fat as a means of preservation. In traditional regional French cooking, duck, goose, and pork are made into confit using fat from the same type of animal. Today, however, it is not uncommon to find other ingredients, such as garlic, tomatoes, and salmon, prepared as confit using various types of fat and not with the aim of preservation.

Deglaze To pour liquid—often wine, stock, or broth—into a pan that has been used to cook foods in order to loosen any browned bits, or *fond*, clinging to the bottom of the pan. The *fond* adds flavor to the liquid, which is then used as a base for a sauce.

Render To cook fat-rich parts of meat or poultry over low to moderate heat in order to cause the fat to melt.

Rest To allow cooked foods, usually fried, seared, roasted, or grilled meat or poultry, to stand for several minutes before cutting or carving. During cooking, natural juices in proteins are pushed toward the center of the cut; resting allows the juices to redistribute throughout the muscle fibers so that the juices do not rapidly flow out when the meat or poultry is cut into.

Roast To cook foods—usually vegetables, poultry, or meats—uncovered in the oven at moderate to high temperatures with the aim of producing a nicely browned exterior and concentrated flavor. A covered gas or charcoal grill can also be used to roast foods; in this case, the technique is referred to as grill-roasting.

Sauté From the French word *sauter*, meaning "to jump." To sauté is to cook food quickly in a shallow pan on the stove top with a small amount of fat, turning it at least once.

Sear To cook foods with moderately high to high heat on the stove top, on a grill, or under a broiler to produce a well-developed crust.

Shock To plunge blanched, boiled, or simmered fruits or vegetables into ice water in order to immediately halt cooking.

Sweat To cook foods, usually diced or sliced vegetables, in a small amount of fat over low to moderate heat until softened but not browned at all.

A Dozen Common Pasta Shapes

1

2

3

4

5

6

cavatappi (1), conchiglie (2), elbow (3), farfalle (4),
fusilli (5), linguine (6), orecchiette (7), penne (8),
ravioli (9), rigatoni (10), spaghetti (11), tortellini (12)

7

8

9

10

11

12

A Few Basic Sauces

Basic sauces, such as hollandaise, chimichurri, and even gravy, are great to have in your culinary repertoire because you can spoon them over ordinary dishes to turn them into extraordinary ones.

Mayonnaise

2 large egg yolks

1 Tbsp fresh lemon juice, plus more as needed

½ tsp Dijon mustard

Salt

1 cup [240 ml] neutral oil

Combine the egg yolks, lemon juice, mustard, and a generous ½ tsp salt in a food processor and process until well mixed. With the machine running, add the oil a few drops at a time to start, gradually increasing to a thin, steady stream. Occasionally stop the machine and scrape the bottom and sides of the bowl. Taste and add more lemon and salt, if needed. If the mayonnaise is too thick, whisk in water, 1 tsp at a time, to thin. Store in an airtight container in the refrigerator for up to 5 days.

MAKES ABOUT 1 ¼ CUPS [300 G]

Lemon-Herb Mayonnaise: Into the finished mayonnaise, stir 1 tsp finely grated lemon zest and ½ cup [20 g] finely chopped mixed tender herbs (such as flat-leaf parsley, chives, basil, dill, or tarragon).

Chipotle Aioli: Omit the mustard, substitute fresh lime juice for the lemon juice, and add 1 Tbsp minced seeded chipotle chile in adobo, 1½ tsp adobo sauce, and 2 minced garlic cloves to the food processor along with the egg yolks, lime juice, and salt.

Hollandaise

½ cup plus 2 Tbsp [140 g] butter, melted and cooled slightly

2 large egg yolks

1 Tbsp fresh lemon juice, plus more as needed

Salt and ground white pepper

Fill a medium saucepan with about 1 in [2.5 cm] of water and set the pan over medium heat. When the water is steaming, turn down the heat to low. Pour the butter into a liquid measuring cup or small pitcher and set it near the stove. In a medium heat-proof bowl that fits onto the saucepan (the water in the pan should not touch the bottom of the bowl), whisk together the egg yolks and lemon juice.

Set the bowl on the pan and whisk the yolk mixture continuously until slightly thickened and lightened in consistency. Whisking constantly, add the butter, a few drops at a time to start, then in the finest stream possible. Check to make sure the water in the pan does not reach a simmer. As the yolk mixture begins to thicken, add the butter in a heavier stream, still whisking constantly. After all the butter has been added, whisk in ½ tsp salt and, if needed, whisk in water to thin the sauce to the desired consistency. Taste and add more salt and lemon juice, if needed, and season with white pepper. Serve immediately.

MAKES ABOUT ¾ CUP [180 ML]

Classic Vinaigrette

3 Tbsp white wine vinegar, red wine vinegar, or Champagne vinegar

1 tsp Dijon mustard

1 Tbsp minced shallot

Salt and ground black pepper

½ cup [120 ml] mild-flavored extra-virgin olive oil

In a small bowl, whisk the vinegar, mustard, shallot, ¼ tsp salt, and ¼ tsp pepper until combined. Gradually whisk in the olive oil. Taste and add more salt and pepper, if needed.

MAKES ABOUT ¾ CUP [180 ML]

Grainy Mustard and Cider Vinaigrette with Maple Syrup: Substitute 2½ Tbsp cider vinegar for the vinegar and 1½ Tbsp whole-grain Dijon mustard for the mustard. Proceed with the recipe, adding 2 tsp maple syrup with the salt and pepper.

Smoked Paprika and Sherry Vinaigrette with Toasted Garlic: Omit the vinegar, mustard, and shallot. In a small, dry skillet over medium-high heat, toast 3 unpeeled garlic cloves, turning them occasionally, until dark brown in spots and softened, about 8 minutes. Remove from the heat and let cool in the skillet. Peel the cloves and, using the back of a fork, mash the garlic with a pinch of salt to a smooth paste. In a small bowl, whisk the garlic paste, 2½ Tbsp sherry vinegar, ½ tsp smoked paprika, ¼ tsp salt, ¼ tsp pepper, and ¼ tsp sugar until combined. Gradually whisk in the olive oil. Taste and add more salt and pepper, if needed.

Poultry Gravy

3 Tbsp butter

2 Tbsp neutral oil

⅓ cup [45 g] Tbsp all-purpose flour

¼ cup [35 g] minced onion

¼ cup [35 g] minced celery

1 garlic clove, lightly smashed and peeled

4 cups [960 ml] low-sodium chicken broth

1 tsp chopped fresh thyme leaves, or ½ tsp dried thyme, crumbled

1 small bay leaf

1½ tsp soy sauce

Salt and ground black pepper

In a medium saucepan, melt the butter with the oil over medium-high heat. Add the flour and cook, whisking constantly, until the mixture (called a *roux*) smells toasty and is medium golden brown, 8 to 9 minutes. Remove the pan from the heat and stir for about 1 minute to cool down the roux. Add the onion, celery, and garlic. Return the pan to medium-high heat and cook, stirring constantly, until the vegetables are softened and the roux is a shade darker, 3 to 4 minutes. Still stirring constantly, gradually pour in the broth. Add the thyme, bay leaf, and soy sauce.

Increase the heat to high, and bring to a boil, stirring constantly. Turn down the heat to medium-high and continue to simmer vigorously, scraping along the sides and bottom of the pan frequently with a silicone spatula, to reduce the sauce. For a medium-light consistency, simmer until the gravy is reduced to about 3 cups [720 ml], about 20 minutes. For a medium-thick consistency, simmer until the gravy is reduced to about 2½ cups [600 ml]. Remove and discard the bay leaf and garlic clove (if the garlic has

cont'd

disintegrated into the gravy, don't worry about it). Season with salt and pepper.

MAKES 2½ TO 3 CUPS [600 TO 720 ML]

Note: The soy sauce adds umami and helps darken the gravy, but won't make the gravy taste like Asian cuisine.

Tomato Sauce with Garlic and Basil

2½ Tbsp extra-virgin olive oil

3 garlic cloves, minced

One 28-oz [794-g] can crushed tomatoes

Salt and ground black pepper

Parmesan rind (optional)

2 to 3 Tbsp chopped fresh basil

In a medium saucepan or large sauté pan, warm 1½ Tbsp of the olive oil and the garlic over medium heat and cook, stirring frequently, until the garlic is no longer raw but not yet browned, 3 to 4 minutes. Pour in the tomatoes and add ½ tsp salt, ¼ tsp pepper, and the Parmesan rind, if using. Stir to combine and bring to a simmer over medium-high heat.

Turn down the heat to medium-low, cover partially, and simmer, stirring occasionally and adjusting the heat as needed, until the sauce is slightly reduced and the flavors have melded, 18 to 20 minutes. Remove and discard the Parmesan rind. Taste and add more salt and pepper, if needed, and stir in the basil and the remaining 1 Tbsp olive oil.

MAKES ABOUT 3 CUPS [720 ML]

Note: For a chunky sauce, use one 28-oz [794-g] can petite diced tomatoes instead of crushed tomatoes; the sauce may require a few minutes of simmering, uncovered, to allow some of the tomato juice to evaporate.

Pesto

2 cups [30 g] packed fresh basil leaves

¼ cup [30 g] pine nuts, lightly toasted (see page 32) and cooled

2 garlic cloves, minced

½ cup [120 ml] extra-virgin olive oil

1 cup [30 g] finely grated Parmesan cheese

Salt and ground black pepper

In a food processor, combine the basil, pine nuts, and garlic and process until very finely chopped, 12 to 15 seconds, stopping once to scrape down the bowl. With the machine running, slowly add the olive oil in a stream, stopping halfway through to scrape down the bowl. Scrape down the bowl again and add the Parmesan, ¼ tsp salt, and ¼ tsp pepper and pulse until well combined. Taste and add more salt and pepper, if needed. (Store the pesto in an airtight container with plastic wrap pressed directly against the surface to prevent discoloration; it will keep for up to 3 days.)

MAKES ABOUT 1 CUP [210 G]

Note: If grating Parmesan on the small holes of a box grater, instead of on a rasp-style grater, use ½ cup [15 g].

Chimichurri

4 garlic cloves

Salt

½ cup [20 g] minced fresh flat-leaf parsley leaves

2 Tbsp minced red onion (optional)

1 tsp red pepper flakes

1½ tsp dried oregano, crumbled

Salt and ground black pepper

½ cup [120 ml] extra-virgin olive oil

¼ cup [60 ml] white wine vinegar

Mince the garlic with a pinch of salt and transfer to a small bowl. Add the parsley, onion (if using), red pepper flakes, oregano, ¾ tsp salt, ¼ tsp pepper, olive oil, and vinegar and whisk to combine. Taste and add more salt and pepper, if needed. Let stand at room temperature for about 30 minutes before using to allow the flavors to meld. (Store leftovers in the refrigerator in an airtight container for up to 2 days; bring to room temperature before serving.)

MAKES ABOUT 1 CUP [240 ML]

Food Storage Tips

Storing foods properly is key to reducing food cost and waste. Here is a basic guide about what goes where and for how long.

Store in the fridge in a container or plastic bag:
Berries (unwashed, up to a week)
Nuts and seeds (up to a year)
Whole-grain flours (up to 6 months)
Nut flours (up to 6 months)
Nut oils and sesame oil (up to a year)
Root vegetables (remove green tops, up to 2 to 3 weeks)
Mint (stand up in water and cover loosely with a plastic bag, up to a week)

Store in the vegetable bin:
Apples (1 to 2 months)
Ripe stone fruit (leave at room temperature until ripe; store up to 5 days)
Ripe tomatoes (leave at room temperature until ripe; store up to a few days)
Ripe avocado (leave at room temperature until ripe; store up to 5 days)
Overripe bananas (skin will darken but fruit will still be edible)

Remove any ties and loosely wrap in a lightly dampened kitchen towel or moistened paper towels. Place in a plastic bag and refrigerate:
Cooking greens (unwashed, up to a week)
Fresh herbs—except basil and mint (up to a week)
Mesclun (unwashed, up to a week)
Lettuce, separated into leaves (up to a week)

...he freezer:
...ts and seeds (up to a year)
Whole-grain flours (up to a year)
Nut flours (up to a year)

**Sealed container in a cool,
dry place in the pantry:**
Refined flours (up to a year)
White rice (indefinitely)
Brown rice (up to a year)*
Whole grains (up to a year)*
Frequently used oils (up to several months)
Shortening (check expiration date)
Onions, shallots, and garlic (up to a few weeks)
Potatoes (up to 2 to 3 weeks)

*For longer storage, or in warm, humid climates,
store in the fridge or freezer

At room temperature:
Basil (stand up in water and cover loosely
   with a plastic bag, up to a week)
Bananas

How Many Cups in a Can

Recipes often call for canned pantry ingredients in volume measurements—cooked beans and tomato products are common ones. Since they come in standard-size cans, it's helpful to know how many cups are in each one. Below you'll find the net volume of a range of products, as well as their net weight when drained, if appropriate.

Note: Net volumes and weights of some products may vary from producer to producer.

Black beans
One 15.5-oz [439-g] can yields 1½ cups [260 g] drained

Cannellini beans
One 15-oz [425-g] can yields 1½ cups [250 g] drained

Kidney beans
One 15.5-oz [439-g] can yields 1½ cups [235 g] drained

Pinto beans
One 15.5-oz [439-g] can yields 1¼ cups [220 g] drained

Chickpeas
One 15.5-oz [439-g] can yields 1½ cups [250 g] drained

Coconut milk
One 13.5-oz [400-ml] can yields 1⅔ cups

Pumpkin purée
One 15-oz [425-g] can yields 1¾ cups

Crushed tomatoes
One 28-oz [794-g] can yields 3⅓ cups

One 14.5-oz [411-g] can yields 1¾ cups

Diced tomatoes
One 28-oz [794-g] can yields 3¼ cups with juice,
2 cups [470 g] drained

One 14.5-oz [411-g] can yields 1¾ cups with juice,
1⅓ cups [300 g] drained

Whole peeled tomatoes
One 28-oz [794-g] can yields 3⅓ cups with juice,
2½ cups [550 g] drained and lightly packed

14.5-oz [411-g] can yields 1½ cups with juice, 1 cup
[245 g] drained and lightly packed

Tomato paste
One 6-oz [170-g] can yields ½ cup plus 2 Tbsp

Tomato sauce
One 8-oz [227-g] can yields 1 cup [240 ml]

One 15-oz [425-g] can yields 1¾ cups [420 ml]